First World War
and Army of Occupation
War Diary
France, Belgium and Germany

30 DIVISION
Divisional Troops
Divisional Trench Mortar Batteries
1 July 1916 - 1 October 1918

WO95/2321/7

The Naval & Military Press Ltd
www.nmarchive.com
Published in association with The National Archives

Published by

The Naval & Military Press Ltd

Unit 10 Ridgewood Industrial Park,

Uckfield, East Sussex,

TN22 5QE England

Tel: +44 (0) 1825 749494

www.naval-military-press.com

www.nmarchive.com

This diary has been reprinted in facsimile from the original. Any imperfections are inevitably reproduced and the quality may fall short of modern type and cartographic standards.

© **Crown Copyright**
Images reproduced by permission of The National Archives, London, England, 2015.

Contents

Document type	Place/Title	Date From	Date To
Heading	30th Division Divl Artillery Trench Mortar Btts. Jun 1917-Oct 1918		
Heading	War Diary. 30th Division Trench Mortars. June, 1917. Volume 20		
War Diary	Watou	01/06/1917	04/06/1917
War Diary	Busseboom	05/06/1917	05/06/1917
War Diary	Zillebeke	06/06/1917	30/06/1917
Heading	War Diary. 30th Divisional Trench Mortars July, 1917. Volume 23		
War Diary	Zillebeke	01/07/1916	30/07/1916
War Diary	Ouderdom & Zillebeke	31/07/1917	31/07/1917
Heading	War Diary. Trench Mortar Batteries 30th Division August, 1917. Volume 22		
War Diary	Ouderdom.	01/08/1917	10/08/1917
War Diary	Bailleul Area.	11/08/1917	15/08/1917
War Diary	Strazeele	16/08/1917	17/08/1917
War Diary	Strazeele Area.	18/08/1917	23/08/1917
War Diary	Dranoutre Area	24/08/1917	31/08/1917
Heading	War Diary. 30th Divisional Trench Mortars. September, 1917 Volume 23		
War Diary	Dranoutre Area.	01/09/1917	30/09/1917
Heading	War Diary 30th Divisional Trench Mortar Batteries October 1917 Volume 24		
War Diary	Dranoutre Area.	01/10/1917	31/10/1917
Heading	Trench Mortar Batteries 30th Divisional Artillery War Diary. Volume.25. November 1917		
War Diary	Dranoutre Area.	01/11/1917	20/11/1917
War Diary	Westoutre Area	21/11/1917	30/11/1917
Heading	Diary Trench Mortar Batts. 30th Divisional Artillery. December, 1917. Volume 26		
War Diary	Westoutre Area	01/12/1917	01/12/1917
War Diary	Cafe Belge	02/12/1917	31/12/1917
Heading	War Diary-30 Division Trench Mortar Batteries Jan 1918 Volume 27		
War Diary	Cafe Belge	01/01/1918	03/01/1918
War Diary	Morbecque	04/01/1918	06/01/1918
War Diary	Rennescure	07/01/1918	09/01/1918
War Diary	Berteaucourt	10/01/1918	12/01/1918
War Diary	Quesnel	13/01/1918	13/01/1918
War Diary	Roiglise	14/01/1918	31/01/1918
Heading	War Diary. T.M. Batteries. 30th Div. Artillery. February 1918. Volume 28		
War Diary	Voyennes	01/02/1918	13/02/1918
War Diary	In Line St Quentin Front.	14/02/1918	14/02/1918
War Diary	In Line St Quentin Area	15/02/1918	28/02/1918
War Diary	Savy (St. Quentin Area)	01/03/1918	15/03/1918
War Diary	Savy	16/03/1918	16/03/1918
War Diary	Savy & Roupy	17/03/1918	31/07/1918
War Diary	In The Field	01/08/1918	10/08/1918
War Diary		01/08/1918	20/08/1918

War Diary		01/08/1918	30/08/1918
War Diary		01/09/1918	30/09/1918
Heading	War Diary Trench Mortar Batteries 30th Div Arty. October 1918 Volume. Vol 17		
War Diary	In The Field	01/10/1918	10/10/1918
War Diary		01/10/1918	20/10/1918
War Diary		01/10/1918	30/10/1918
War Diary		01/10/1918	01/10/1918

30TH DIVISION
DIVL ARTILLERY

TRENCH MORTAR BTTS.
JUN 1917 — OCT 1918

30TH DIVISION
DIVL ARTILLERY

WAR DIARY.

30th DIVISION — TRENCH MORTARS.

June 1917

VOLUME 20.

Oct 1918

WAR DIARY or INTELLIGENCE SUMMARY.

30th Division TRENCH MORTARS Army Form C. 2118.

(Erase heading not required.)

Hour, Date, Place		Summary of Events and Information	Remarks and references to Appendices
1-6-17	WATOU	Received four 9-45" Mortars from DADOS. One Mortar not fit for action being damaged by shell fire.	
2-6-17	do.	Received instructions to put Two Medium T.M. Batteries in the line	
3-6-17	do.	OTM.O. went forward to reconnoitre for Medium positions with OC/ V/30 & Y/30 and Z/30. The trench system was in very bad condition & most emplacements were already existed & owing to water it was found that it would be impossible to dig the emplacements any depth.	
4-6-17	do.	All TM Batteries marched up from WATOU to BUSSEBOOM & were accommodated with the DAC in Tents.	
5-6-17	BUSSEBOOM	Y & Z Batteries moved up to ZILLEBEKE area. V/30 & X/30 remained at BUSSEBOOM.	
6-6-17	ZILLEBEKE	Work was started on Medium emplacements.	
7-6-17	do	Batteries were heavily shelled with HE & gas shells in ZILLEBEKE and infortunately suffered casualties. Both Officers of Y/30 Lieut F.E Wenrul & 2/Lieut H.M Fletcher being killed. 3 ORs and 4 ORs wounded in Z/30	

WAR DIARY or INTELLIGENCE SUMMARY

Army Form C. 2118.

Hour, Date, Place	Summary of Events and Information	Remarks and references to Appendices
8-6-17 ZILLEBEKE	The two medium batteries moved from ZILLEBEKE to the S. side of ZILLEBEKE LAKE & dug themselves in under the bank. 150 infantry Carrying party carried bombs from ZILLEBEKE to the positions.	
9-6-17 do	Work continued on medium emplacements. Went down to V/30 with 50 men joined Y & Z Batteries to assist with the work in hand.	
10-6-17 do	The Batteries were shelled with gas shells one man from each Battery being admitted to hospital.	
11-6-17 do	Work was continued on the emplacements.	
12-6-17 do	Two 2 O.R.s of X/30 who came up to replace casualties in the other Batteries were wounded. 4 O.R.s of Y/30 admitted to hospital suffering from the effects of gas.	
13-6-17 do	Work on Emplacements continued. Ammunition was carried forward & carrying party of 150 infantry men & one ammunition van again carried up to the positions.	
14-6-17 do	V/30 & X/30 moved from BUSSEBOOM to OUDERDOM area – 3 O.R.s of V/30 slightly wounded still at duty.	

WAR DIARY
or
INTELLIGENCE SUMMARY.
(Erase heading not required.)

Army Form C. 2118.

Hour, Date, Place		Summary of Events and Information	Remarks and references to Appendices
16-6-17	ZILLEBEKE	Work continued – 1 O.R. of Y/30 wounded	
17-6-17	do.	Work continued	
18-6-17	do.	Received instruction to build emplacements for 4 9·45" T.M's	
19-6-17	do.	D.T.M.O. went forward to reconnoitre positions for the 9·45" with OC Y/30 and OC 201st Field Coy. Lieut Watson of 2/30 was made the Military Cross.	
20-6-17	do.	Y/30 moved up into the forward area. Work was continued a building emplacements – Lieut Watson 2/30 was slightly wounded + 1 OR of Y/30 killed whilst at duty.	
21-6-17	do.	1 OR of 2/30 wounded. Work on 9·45" emplacements. It was arranged to shoot Y/30 the following day, that covering fire	
22-6-17	do.	should be given by the Field Batteries.	
23-6-17	do.	Y/30 fired 20 rounds & enemy were silenced. The 113 Bde RFA put up covering fire from two Batteries	
24-6-17	do.	Work continued – Y/30 was shelled out of the S side of the ZILLEBEKE LAKE & moved forward into the tunnel on OBSERVATORY RIDGE.	
25-6-17	do.	1 OR of 2/30 wounded	

Army Form C. 2118.

WAR DIARY
or
INTELLIGENCE SUMMARY.
(Erase heading not required.)

Instructions regarding War Diaries and Intelligence Summaries are contained in F.S. Regs., Part II. and the Staff Manual respectively. Title pages will be prepared in manuscript.

Hour, Date, Place		Summary of Events and Information	Remarks and references to Appendices
26-6-17	ZILLEBEKE	Received instructions for Y/30 to shoot in conjunction with Heavy Artillery. This was cancelled later. 1 O.R. of 2/30 wounded.	
27-6-17	do		
28-6-17	do	2/30 came 4 out of the line to OUDERDOM to rest, leaving 1 medium Battery in the line. 1 O.R. 2/30 wounded.	
29-6-17	do	D.T.M.O. took 2 Lieut Bruxson sent to E Army Trench Mortar School to see first shoot with 6" Stokes.	
30-6-17	do	C.R.A. went round the Heavy emplacements being built in the line. 5 O.R's of V/30 went to E Army T.M. School for instruction on the 6" Stokes. Arrangements were made for the 113 Bde R.F.A. to supply the T.M's with a working party of 1 Officer & 60 O.R. to report on the night of 1st July.	

R.B. Moore Capt R.A.
D.T.M.O. 30 Div

No 2

WAR DIARY.

30th Divisional Trench Mortars

JULY, 1917

VOLUME 23.

WAR DIARY of 30th Divisional TRENCH MORTARS

Army Form C. 2118.

INTELLIGENCE SUMMARY

(Erase heading not required.)

Hour, Date, Place		Summary of Events and Information	Remarks and references to Appendices
1-7-16	ZILLEBEKE	Received two 6" Stokes mortars and two 9-45" (new pattern long) from D.A.D.O.S.	
2-7-16	do	Fine day. Work was continued on the 9-45" & medium emplacements.	
3-7-16	do	DTMO with Capt B/S Ellis went to 2d Army T.M. School to obtain plans of new bed for 6" Newton and also to see it.	
4-7-17	do	Filled up this day with a class, most of the day. AE material was carried up to emplacements & work continued	
5-7-17	do	Received instructions that 2d Australian J.A. T.M's had been allotted to the Division. Shelter for started work on position for 6" Newton work on their emplacements	
6-7-17	do		
7-7-17	do	1 officer & 60 ORs started to the Batteries for work left to rejoin their Brigade (158)	
8-7-17	do	2d Australian J.A. T.M's arrived & were located a field with 16 tents near OUDERDOM. They not to take same fire line	

WAR DIARY
or
INTELLIGENCE SUMMARY.
(Erase heading not required.)

Army Form C. 2118.

Hour, Date, Place		Summary of Events and Information	Remarks and references to Appendices
9-7-17	ZILLEBEKE.	2nd Australian T.M's sent one medium Battery & half of their Heavy Battery into the line. The heavies starts to build up position for the new Heavy Mortars.	
10-7-17	do.	D.T.M.O. 2nd Australian Div reconnoitred the positions with D.T.M.O 30 Div. Fine day.	
11-7-17	do.	Orders were received that the 2" mortar entrance in conjunction with the 6" howrs. two 2 offensives postponed. Lieut Rattlett was slightly wounded in the face remaining still at duty.	
12-7-17	do.	The 18th Div. T.M's marched in & were billetted. W.J. Dickiebusch. The 2" Battery in the line fired 15 rounds on enemy's wire.	
13-7-17	do.	The 18th Division lent forward one officer & 16 men to hold position for 6" Morton. 500 rounds of ammunition taken up by D.A.C for 6" Morton. 2" Batteries fired 76 rounds on enemy's wire with good results.	
14-7-17	do.	The 2nd Australian & 30th Division 2" Batteries fired 162 rounds on enemy's wire front-line with excellent results.	

WAR DIARY
or
INTELLIGENCE SUMMARY.
(Erase heading not required.)

Army Form C. 2118.

Hour, Date, Place	Summary of Events and Information	Remarks and references to Appendices
15-7-17 ZILLEBEKE	2" Australian Medium Battery was relieved in the line by 2/18 Battery. The 2" fired 32 rounds on enemy's wire. Carrying party was supplied by Infantry	
16-7-17 do.	The 2" continued wire cutting firing 51 rounds. 1/30 got our heavy T.M. into the line and also 2 six inch heavy guns. Lieut Keenan sent on leave.	
17-7-17 do.	The 2" Batteries had 3 positions than in hore-ammeter stook one immediately station between them. 12 2" rounds were fired. took control of 9.45 & 6" Positions	
18-7-17 do	Bad weather. Ammunition too wet to get up to ZILLEBEKE. 2" fired 26 rounds on enemy's wire. 2" Australian TMs handed over to 24Div. the 1st A.T.M's 10 in no.	
19-7-17 do	Lieut Baxter took 2/30 into the line. 2" Batteries fired 133 rounds. Both the 6" emplacements were cutting and damaging enemy's front line by hostile shell fire. Under construction were blown in by hostile shell fire.	
20-7-17 do.	The 2" Batteries fired 76 rounds. Not too sure on repairing damage. 6" Howr. emplacements.	
21-7-17 do	The 2" Battery fired 146 rounds on enemy's front line with good effect. The 6" howrs was fired for the first time. 1.30 rounds were expended with very satisfactory results. The 9.45" fired 19 rounds.	

WAR DIARY
or
INTELLIGENCE SUMMARY.
(Erase heading not required.)

Army Form C. 2118.

Hour, Date, Place	Summary of Events and Information	Remarks and references to Appendices
22-7-17 ZILLEBEKE	The 2" T.M's fired 114 rounds, innoculating the 6" Newton 64 rounds.	
23-7-17 do.	The 2" fired 90 rounds & the 6" 75 rounds. One 6" gun was changed by hostile shell fire.	
24-7-17 do.	Lieut Bartlett took up Y/30 Battery to dug out near SHRAPNEL CORNER to help with the carrying of 2" ammunition. Lieut Radford returned from hospital. 2" fired 96 rounds & 6" Newton 68 rounds. Infantry carrying party for ammunition supplies.	
25-7-17 do.	Lieut Davison took up to Q V/30 which was at the line to help with the carrying of ammunition for the heavy Battery. The 2" fired 82 rounds & the 6" Newton 115 rounds. Patrols report very little was along the whole front line. Guns had received orders at 1 am on attack to the Infantry. Heavy rain fell during the morning. Infantry carrying party was supplied.	
26-7-17 do.	The 2" Batteries fired 64 rounds & the 6" Newton 70 rounds. A successful daylight raid was carried out by our Division. The leading party of wire that was was well cut all along front. Lieut Barton was slightly wounded remaining at duty. A few but dull day. Infantry carrying party was supplied.	
27-7-17 do.	Beautiful day good observation. Infantry carrying party was supplied in the early morning. The 2" Batteries fired 240 rounds & Germans much damage to enemy wire & trenches. The 6" Newton fired 73 rounds.	
28-7-17 do.	Fine hot day. Lieut Bartlett brought Y/30 Battery, which has been up carrying, out of the line. V/30 suffered 2 casualties. The dug out in Railway Embankment was blown in & buried 1 Sgt 2 Corporals & 1 O.R. The latter was dug out badly bruised about the face & taken to hospital but unfortunately the other 2 were killed.	

WAR DIARY
or
INTELLIGENCE SUMMARY.
(Erase heading not required.)

Army Form C. 2118.

Hour, Date, Place	Summary of Events and Information	Remarks and references to Appendices
29-7-17 ZILLEBEKE	Heavy Thunder storm raining most of the morning. The 2" fired 62 rounds after which the emplacements became too bad to do any further firing owing to the heavy rain. The 6" Newton was blown in by hostile shell fire.	
30-7-17 do	Fine but very dull day. 6" Newton fired 100 rounds. The 2" Batteries withdrew their personnel back to the Camp near OUDERDOM leaving a guard over the guns.	
31-7-17 OUDERDOM & ZILLEBEKE	Zero day. Very dull day into rain at night. 1/30 H.Battery withdrew personnel to Camp at OUDERDOM leaving guard over guns in the line.	

R.W.W. Capt RA
T.M. 30 Div

Vol 3

WAR DIARY.

Trench Mortar Batteries 30th Division

August, 1917.

Volume 22

30th Division TRENCH MORTARS

Army Form C. 2118.

WAR DIARY
or
INTELLIGENCE SUMMARY.
(Erase heading not required.)

Instructions regarding War Diaries and Intelligence Summaries are contained in F.S. Regs., Part II and the Staff Manual respectively. Title pages will be prepared in manuscript.

Hour, Date, Place		Summary of Events and Information	Remarks and references to Appendices
1-8-17	OUDERDOM	Very bad day, heavy rain until night. 44 men were sent from the Batteries to help the 30th D.A.C. unloading.	
2-8-17	do	Dull day - much colder. Each Battery sent parties forward to collect guns and stores.	
3-8-17	do	Very wet & cold day. Parties remained in the line trying to the great difficulty of getting the guns out. The pits being full of water & the guns having been in action.	
4-8-17	do	Better weather. Parties shown in afternoon. One G.S. wagon sent up the line to bring 7 2" mortars which had been recovered from the line. Party remained to recover 3 other guns which has been buried by shell fire & bad weather.	
5-8-17	do	T.M. Batteries resting. The 3 2" mortars were recovered from the line. The broken pieces of the 9.45" T.M. were also brought down from the line but owing to the bad state of the ground to 6" Newtons had to be left. 2/Lt Knight proceeded to X/30 wire Lieut Gilmore evacuated to England. Fine day.	
6-8-17	do	Received instruction to hand over to the 56th Division 4 9.45" mortars 2 9.45" (long) mortars & 2 6" Newtons prior to our departure from this area. Fine.	
7-8-17	do		

Army Form C. 2118.

WAR DIARY
or
INTELLIGENCE SUMMARY.
(Erase heading not required.)

Instructions regarding War Diaries and Intelligence
Summaries are contained in F. S. Regs., Part II
and the Staff Manual respectively. Title pages
will be prepared in manuscript.

Hour, Date, Place		Summary of Events and Information	Remarks and references to Appendices
8-8-17	OUDERDOM.	Fine day. 6" Newtons were handed out by the line. Bttns.	
9-8-17	do	Fine but cloudy day. Handed over heavy & 6" TM's to 56th Division	
10-8-17	do	Fine day.	
11-8-17	BAILLEUL AREA.	The trench mortars moved in lorries from OUDERDOM to BAILLEUL AREA. Fine day with a few showers.	
12-8-17	do	Showery day	
13-8-17	do	do	
14-8-17	do	do	
15-8-17	do	Trench mortars move from BAILLEUL Area to STRAZEELE Area, & were encamped with the D.A.C.	
16-8-17	STRAZEELE	Fine day	
17-8-17	do	do	

30F Division TRENCH MORTARS

Army Form C. 2118.

WAR DIARY
or
INTELLIGENCE SUMMARY.
(Erase heading not required.)

Instructions regarding War Diaries and Intelligence Summaries are contained in F.S. Regs., Part II. and the Staff Manual respectively. Title pages will be prepared in manuscript.

Hour, Date, Place		Summary of Events and Information	Remarks and references to Appendices
18-8-17	STRAZEELE AREA.	Sunday Service	
19-8-17	STRAZEELE AREA	Fine day. Batteries cooking & helping DAC.	
20-8-17	do.	do	
21-8-17	do.	do	
22-8-17	do	do	
23-8-17	do	T.M. School & Army for short course of instruction. Lieut Bartlett took 10 O.R.s to 6" Mortar. Fine day with a few showers late in the afternoon & evening. The Batteries left Strata.	
24-8-17	MANDOUTRE AREA	The T.M.'s moved with DAC to the MANDOUTRE AREA, 10 O.R.s were sent from the Batteries to be attached to the 3 Sections of the D.A.C. Lieuts Burton, Herring and Radford returned from leave.	

WAR DIARY
or
INTELLIGENCE SUMMARY.
(Erase heading not required.)

Army Form C. 2118.

Hour, Date, Place	Summary of Events and Information	Remarks and references to Appendices
25-8-17 DRANOUTRE AREA	30th French Artans took over ammunition for 4½ Australian Div.	
26-8-17 do	They have no guns in the line — Fine day	
27-8-17 do	Actively hot night	
28-8-17 do	Last ammunition	
29-8-17 do	Fine hot unpounder	
30-8-17 do	Handed over ammunition to 14th Div. having given up the Southern portion of our Divl. front. Took over 2 howies & 2 6" Newton from 37th Div. Two of these has to be sent to Ord. for repairs.	
31-8-17		

W. Orr Capt.
D. T. M. O. Granville

Vol 4

WAR DIARY.

30th Divisional Trench Mortars.

September, 1917.

Volume 23.

30th Division TRENCH MORTARS.

Army Form C. 2118.

WAR DIARY
or
INTELLIGENCE SUMMARY.
(Erase heading not required.)

Instructions regarding War Diaries and Intelligence Summaries are contained in F.S. Regs., Part II. and the Staff Manual respectively. Title pages will be prepared in manuscript.

Hour, Date, Place	Summary of Events and Information	Remarks and references to Appendices
DRANOUTRE AREA. 1-9-17	A fine day. Lieut Bartlett was sent to D/149 & Lieut Radford to C/148 to be attached.	
do. 2-9-17	A fine day. Lieut Sergt Lawson went on leave.	
do. 3-9-17	Division handed over the Southern sector of their front to 14th Division & took over an extra portion of the line further North from the 37th Division. Two 9.45" MKI TMs were taken over from 37th Division & sent to one other, also one 9.45" MKII.	
do. 4-9-17	Capt B.W. Ellis rejoined from leave. Beautiful day, much aerial activity.	
do. 5-9-17	Lieut Knight rejoined from leave.	
do. 6-9-17	Took over 42 rounds 9.45" ammunition and 168 rounds of 6" ammunition from 37th Division Trench Mortars. Fine morning, very heavy thunder storm in the afternoon.	
do. 7-9-17	Fine hot heavy days	
do. 8-9-17	do	
do. 9-9-17	do	
do. 10-9-17	Fine hot days	

Army Form C. 2118.

WAR DIARY
or
INTELLIGENCE SUMMARY
(Erase heading not required.)

Instructions regarding War Diaries and Intelligence Summaries are contained in F.S. Regs., Part II. and the Staff Manual respectively. Title Pages will be prepared in manuscript.

Place	Date	Hour	Summary of Events and Information	Remarks and references to Appendices
DRANOUTRE AREA	11-9-17	—	Fine day - quiet.	
do	12-9-17	—	A further portion of the line was taken over by the Division from the 37th Division. No Trench Mortar base in this portion of the front.	
do	13-9-17	—	Fine day.	
do	14-9-17	—	Lt. Walsh of V/30 Battery went on leave.	
do	15-9-17	—	D.T.M.O. & Capt Ellis went up to find a suitable site to put a 6" Newton. All possible positions were at long ranges.	
do	16-9-17	—	Lieut. Samson V/30 Battery returned from leave - Fine day.	
do	17-9-17	—	Received gun from Ordnance 9.45" MkI. Capt Ellis took forward 12 men to start work on a 6" emplacement - Fine day.	
do	18-9-17	—	Fine day.	
do	19-9-17	—	do	
do	20-9-17	—	Fine day. One 6" Newton taken up to be position.	
do	21-9-17	—	Fine day.	

Army Form C. 2118.

WAR DIARY
or
INTELLIGENCE SUMMARY
(Erase heading not required.)

Place	Date	Hour	Summary of Events and Information	Remarks and references to Appendices
DRANOUTRE AREA	22-9-17	—	Fine day.	
do	23-9-17	—	Fine day — 10 Rounds were fired for the purpose of registration of the 6" howitzer position.	
do	24-9-17	—	Fine day — 80 rounds taken up to position at night.	
do	25-9-17	—	Fine day. Lt. Austin returned from leave — his firing was done at the request of the Infantry.	
do	26-9-17	—	Fine day. X/30 was relieved by Y/30 Battery.	
do	27-9-17	—	Fine day. The following Officers were attached to the 30 D.A.C. Lt Watson & 2Lts Rosford, Austin & Samson —	
do	28-9-17	—	Reconnoitres for new 6" Emplacement in Southern Sector of Divisional Front. One possible Emplacement was found off MANCHESTER TRENCH.	
do	29-9-17	—	Fine day.	
do	30-9-17	—	Fine day.	

R. Spence Capt.
O/C 30 D/A

Ya 5 War Diary

20th Division
Trench Mortar Batteries

October 1917

Volume 24

30th Division TRENCH MORTAR BATTERIES.

Army Form C. 2118.

WAR DIARY
or
INTELLIGENCE SUMMARY
(Erase heading not required.)

Instructions regarding War Diaries and Intelligence Summaries are contained in F. S. Regs., Part II. and the Staff Manual respectively. Title Pages will be prepared in manuscript.

Place	Date	Hour	Summary of Events and Information	Remarks and references to Appendices
DRANOUTRE AREA.	1-10-17		Fine day. During the night there was great aerial activity. Many bombs were dropped by hostile aeroplanes.	
do.	2-10-17		Fine day. Lieut Arnott was temporarily attached to D/148 Bany to the casualties to officers this Battery has suffered the previous night.	
do.	3-10-17		Rain in early morning, fine later.	
do.	4-10-17		Fine with showers.	
do.	5-10-17		Wet day, very quiet. Lieut Pittman with 25 men from TM Batte: stales took a wagon line for Brigade for Winter.	
do.	6-10-17		The 6" Newton fired 20 rounds on "The Twins".	
do.	7-10-17		Reconnoitred possible position for the another 6" Newton T.M. off MANCHESTER TRENCH. Very wet & cold day.	
do.	8-10-17		Thirty more men from the TM Batteries were attached to Lieut P. Herman to work on the winter standings for wagon lines. Very wet & stormy afternoon & during the night.	
do.	9-10-17		Showery & very windy.	
do.	10-10-17		Quiet day. Showery.	
do.	11-10-17		-do- -do-	

WAR DIARY or INTELLIGENCE SUMMARY

Army Form C. 2118.

Place	Date	Hour	Summary of Events and Information	Remarks and references to Appendices
DRANOUTRE AREA	12-10-17		Wet day. Ammunition for 6" Newton T.M. was taken forward.	
do.	13-10-17		Wet day. Capt B.W. Ellis V/30 went on leave to Rouen for 4 days.	
do.	14-10-17		X/30 fired 20 rounds on the Twins with the 6" Newton T.M. a fine day	
do.	15-10-17		Fine day.	
do.	16-10-17		X/30 fired 11 rounds with good effect with the 6" Newton. Fine day.	
do.	17-10-17		X/30 fired 15 rounds on machine gun emplacement & enemy's posts.	
do.	18-10-17		Ammunition taken up for 6" Newton.	
do.	19-10-17		Fine day. D.T.M.O reconnoitred for position for 9.45" T.M. (long). Owing to the forward slope there were very few available positions.	
do.	20-10-17		Fine day. Shoot taken in the day. Capt B.W.Ellis was put in charge of Ammunition Dump while the officer of the dump was on leave.	
do.	21-10-17		Dull day.	
do.	22-10-17		X/30 fired 25 rounds with the 6" T.M. on enemy's posts.	
do.	23-10-17			
do.	24-10-17		Fine day. G.O.A went round the forward area to see the T.M. emplacements and also to fix on a site for the 9.45" T.M.(long). A good position was selected but the Div.Commander would not allow it to be made use of as it was too close to Infantry Bttg. H.Q.	

Army Form C. 2118.

WAR DIARY
or
INTELLIGENCE SUMMARY
(Erase heading not required.)

Instructions regarding War Diaries and Intelligence Summaries are contained in F. S. Regs., Part II and the Staff Manual respectively. Title pages will be prepared in manuscript.

Place	Date	Hour	Summary of Events and Information	Remarks and references to Appendices
DRANOUTRE AREA.	25-10-17		Fine day. X/30 fired again with the 6" howitzer with good results.	
do.	26-10-17		Very wet day.	
do.	27-10-17		X/30 fired the 6" howitzer on enemy's posts.	
do.	28-10-17		Fine day. Quiet. Ammunition was taken up at night.	
do.	29-10-17		Fine day. The 6" howitzer was again fired on the GIANTS and TWINS and enemy's posts.	
do.	30-10-17		Fine in early morning very wet later in day. Capt. Bur. Ellis was appointed DADOS of the 8th Division.	
do.	31-10-17		Fine day.	

Trench Mortar Batteries
30th Divisional Artillery

War Diary.

Volume 25

November 1917.

WAR DIARY
or
INTELLIGENCE SUMMARY
(Erase heading not required.)

Army Form C. 2118.
30th Division Trench Mortar Battery

Place	Date	Hour	Summary of Events and Information	Remarks and references to Appendices
DRANOUTRE AREA.	1-11-17		Fine. 6" Newton was unable to fire in accordance with programme owing to the bed having slipped due to the very wet state of the ground.	
"	2-11-17		Capt. B.W. Ellis joined the 8th Division to take up the Duties of D.T.M.O.	
"	3-11-17		Fine day.	
"	4-11-17		Fine day.	
"	5-11-17		Fine day.	
"	6-11-17		Wet day.	
"	7-11-17		Wet day.	
"	8-11-17		Fine day. X/30 Battery fired 72 rounds 6" Newton with good results.	
"	9-11-17		Fine day.	
"	10-11-17		Wet day. Fired 20 rounds with 6" Newton from new position in Kransestter Street.	
"	11-11-17		Wet day.	
"	12-11-17		Fine day.	
"	13-11-17		Fine day. A German medium Trench Mortar which was found was brought out of Huns	
"	14-11-17		Fine day.	
"	15-11-17		Fine day. D.T.M.O. 5th Australian Division came over to see the Camp and position which they were to take over.	
"	16-11-17		Dull day. D.T.M.O. went on leave to England. Lieut G.E. Barton acting in his absence.	
"	17-11-17		X/30 relieved by 5th Australian TM Battery & were withdrawn to Camp at Dranoutre with the other Batteries.	
"	18-11-17		Fine day. V/30 handed over 9.45" guns & stores to 5th Australian Trench Mortar Batteries resting at Camp at DRANOUTRE	

WAR DIARY
or
INTELLIGENCE SUMMARY
(Erase heading not required.)

Army Form C. 2118.

Place	Date	Hour	Summary of Events and Information	Remarks and references to Appendices
DRANOUTRE AREA	19-11-17	Fine day	Lieut P. Heenan sent to WESTOUTRE AREA to take over trench mortars from the 39th Division (2 6" and 1 9·45" M/k III)	
do.	20-11-17	Fine day	Advance party reported to Lieut Heenan (2 men from each Battery)	
WESTOUTRE AREA	21-11-17	Rained all day	T.M. Batteries moved to WESTOUTRE AREA. Lieut Watson and 2nd Lieut Radford rejoined from the D.A.C.	
do	22-11-17	Wet day		
	23-11-17	Fine day		
	24-11-17	Fine day		
	25-11-17	Wet day	O.C. 1/30 reconnoitred for position for 9·45" M/k III	
	26-11-17	Wet day		
	27-11-17	Wet day	Fired 2 rounds from the 9·45" Mark III to test the Bed which proved to be unsatisfactory. It was decided to relay the platform	
	28-11-17	Fine day		
	29-11-17	Fine day	Baths were arranged for the personnel of the Batteries for the 1st proxo.	
	30-11-17	Fine day	D.A.D.M.S. 30th Division lent his hired cart to the T.M. Batteries.	

Murray Capt
M. O. 30th

WAR DIARY

Trench Mortar Batts.
30th Divisional Artillery

December, 1917.

Volume 26.

Army Form C. 2118.

WAR DIARY
or
INTELLIGENCE SUMMARY

(Erase heading not required.)

TRENCH MORTAR BATTERIES
30th DIVISION

Instructions regarding War Diaries and Intelligence Summaries are contained in F. S. Regs., Part II and the Staff Manual respectively. Title Pages will be prepared in manuscript.

Place	Date	Hour	Summary of Events and Information	Remarks and references to Appendices
WESTOUTRE AREA	1-12-17		Dull and stormy. Baths for personnel of the T.M. Batteries. Transport was arranged to move the Batteries to CAFÉ BELGE on 2nd inst. D.T.M.O. returned from leave. Y/30 Battery fired 20 rounds with 6" howitzer.	
CAFÉ BELGE	2-12-17		Fine day, thaw kind. 2/Lieut. J.A.E. Lawson returned from course of Gunnery. The Batteries moved forward to CAFÉ BELGE and were billeted in wooden huts.	
do.	3-12-17		Fine cold day.	
do.	4-12-17		Fine day, frosty. D.T.M.O. went round the T.M. emplacements and reconnoitred for alternative positions. Arrangements made for 2/Lt. Humphries to be posted to V/30 vice Lieut. Austin to be posted to D/148 Bde RFA	
do.	5-12-17		Fine frosty day.	
do.	6-12-17		Fine frosty. Arrangements were made for him to carry 5 officers and 12 NCO's vice to Army T.M. School on the 7th inst. for a demonstration shoot with the 6" howitzer T.M.	
do.	7-12-17		Fine dull. Demonstration with the 6" howitzer T.M. at T.M. School. C.R.A. and Brigade Majors attended also D.T.M.O. and Officers NCO's and men from the T.M. Batteries. Arrangements made with the 30th D.A.C. to take at least two men from each Battery on the 8th inst. and instruct them in signalling and elephant's duties.	
do.	8-12-17		Fine day mild. Received orders for 9.45" MkII at DICKEBUSCH Railhead - Arranged for two G.S. wagons from D.A.C. to Loading party from V/30 to clean same.	
do.	9-12-17		Very wet day. Quiet on front - D.T.M.O. went up to select new position for 6" T.M.	
do.	10-12-17		Fine day.	

WAR DIARY or INTELLIGENCE SUMMARY

Army Form C. 2118.

Place	Date	Hour	Summary of Events and Information	Remarks and references to Appendices
CAFE BELGE	11-12-17		Dull and cold day. V/30 Battery took the Subsd for 9.45" T.M. up to the position at INVERNESS COPSE at 4 a.m. Three F.S. Wagons from the D.A.C. were lent for this purpose. 2 Lieut Humphreys joined V/30 Battery.	
do.	12-12-17		Fine day. 2nd Lieut A.H. Blutton of D.A.C. returned from IV Army T.M. School and was posted to X/30 Battery.	
do.	13-12-17		Fine dull. Work was continued on construction of 9.45" and 6" emplacements and improvement of Camp.	
do.	14-12-17		2nd Lieut A.H. Blutton joined X/30 Battery. Dull day with little rain. Lieut G.T. Boxton went on leave to England. 2 Lieut J.A.C. Samson who had been attached to D.A.C. rejoined V/30 Battery to take charge while Lieut Boxton was away. X/30 Battery relieved Z/30 Battery in the line.	
do.	15-12-17		Fine day. Ammunition was carried forward to the 6" emplacements.	
do.	16-12-17		Cold day. One 6" T.M. emplacement was hit during the day but the hut was completely destroyed.	
do.	17-12-17		Snow in early morning. Fine later.	
do.	18-12-17		Fine and frosty.	
do.	19-12-17		Fine and frosty. 150 rounds 6" ammunition were taken up in early morning to INVERNESS COPSE by limber G.S. Wagons also hurried to replace one destroyed. V/30 Battery fired from his 6" position.	
do.	20-12-17		Frosty and thick mist all day. 6" ammunition was carried forward to the position by Z/30 and V/30 Batteries. Work was continued on the 9.45" (in) T.M. position, fitting the shelves.	
do.	21-12-17		Frosty. The 6" howitzer T.M. fired on LEWIS HOUSE – observation was bad.	
do.	22-12-17		Fine day/ morning.	

WAR DIARY
or
INTELLIGENCE SUMMARY

(Erase heading not required.)

Army Form C. 2118.

Place	Date	Hour	Summary of Events and Information	Remarks and references to Appendices
CAFE BELGE	23-12-17		Fine, frosty. C.R.A. & R.O. twisted the T.M. emplacements with the D.T.M.O. Y/30 fired 28 rounds with the 6" trench mortar.	
do	24-12-17		Fine morning, rain in afternoon. 100 rounds 6" ammunition were taken up to forward dump at dusk. Y/30 Battery supplied carrying party to take the ammunition forward to 6" emplacements.	
do	25-12-17		Fine, snow later in day. All men came back to CAMP at CAFE BELGE for Xmas dinner.	
do	26-12-17		Snow storms - Quiet day.	
do	27-12-17		Fine. Snow on ground - no shooting done.	
do	28-12-17		Fine frost.	
do	29-12-17		Fine frost. Received training order that be Bde Arty. would be relieved about the 5th Jan by 37 Div Arty.	
do	30-12-17		Fine frosty.	
do	31-12-17		Fine frosty. Capt E.T. Baxter Y/30 Battery returned from leave.	

J. W. Carpenter
D.T.O. 30th Div
1-1-18.

WAR DIARY —

1918

30 Division Trench Mortar Batteries

Jan 1918   Volume 27.

SECRET

Army Form C. 2118.

WAR DIARY
30th DIVISION TRENCH MORTAR BATTERIES.

INTELLIGENCE SUMMARY
(Erase heading not required.)

Instructions regarding War Diaries and Intelligence Summaries are contained in F. S. Regs., Part II. and the Staff Manual respectively. Title Pages will be prepared in manuscript.

Place	Date	Hour	Summary of Events and Information	Remarks and references to Appendices
CAFE BELGE	1-1-18		Fine & frosty. D.T.M.O. 37th Division came over to arrange about relief.	
do.	2-1-18		Fine & frosty. Officers from 37th Division T.M. Batteries took over guns & emplacements & ammunition.	
do.	3-1-18		Fine & frosty. Lorries were provided to move the T.M. Batteries to MORBECQUE where they were billetted. Relief complete.	
MORBECQUE	4-1-18		Fine & frosty. Batteries resting in MORBECQUE.	
do.	5-1-18		do.	
do.	6-1-18		Batteries were moved by lorries to RENNESCURE & billetted there.	
RENNESCURE	7-1-18		Fine & slight thaw. Batteries resting at RENNESCURE. Received orders for entrainment.	
RENNESCURE	8-1-18		Frosty. X/30 Battery entrained at STEENBECQUE at midday detrained at LONGEAU. Lorry provided to move stores to BERTEAUCOURT. Other Batteries remained at RENNESCURE.	
RENNESCURE	9-1-18		Fine & frosty. V/30 entrained at STEENBECQUE followed by V/30 & Z/30. Heavy loss.	
BERTEAUCOURT	10-1-18		Fine & frosty. V, Y, & Z/30 Batteries marched from LONGEAU to BERTEAUCOURT & were billetted there.	
do.	11-1-18		Fine. Resting at BERTEAUCOURT.	
do.	12-1-18		Fine thaw. Batteries marched to QUESNEL & billetted there. G.S. wagons were provided for stores. Lieut HEENAN and	
QUESNEL	13-1-18		Night went on leave.	
ROIGLISE	14-1-18		Fine & frosty. Batteries marched from QUESNEL to ROIGLISE. G.S. wagons provided for the move.	
do.	15-1-18		Fine & frosty. Batteries resting.	
do.	16-1-18			
do.	17-1-18		Batteries resting & fitting & training.	
do.	18-1-18			
do.	19-1-18			
do.	20-1-18			

WAR DIARY
or
INTELLIGENCE SUMMARY

(Erase heading not required.)

Army Form C. 2118.

Place	Date	Hour	Summary of Events and Information	Remarks and references to Appendices
ROIGLISE	21-1-18		Wet morning, fine later.	
do	22-1-18		Fine, dull a.m.	
do	23-1-18		Fine, mild	Batteries resting, refitting & training.
do	24-1-18		Foggy morning, fine later	
do	25-1-18		do do	
do	26-1-18		do do	
do	27-1-18		Fine, foggy in morning.	Batteries moved from ROIGLISE to VOYENNES by lorries & have billets there.
do	28-1-18		Fine frosty morning.	Received instructions to re-organise the T.M. personnel & form two new Sub-sim Batteries
do	29-1-18		do do	Personnel were paraded & allotted to each battery. Lieut Heenan & Knight returned from leave.
do	30-1-18		do do	Lieut Dawson went on leave
do	31-1-18		Frost in morning, dull day.	

[signature] Capt.
31/1/18

WAR DIARY.

T.M. BATTERIES,
30th DIV. ARTILLERY.

February 1918.

Volume 28

Vol 9

WAR DIARY 30th DIVISION TRENCH MORTAR BATTERIES Army Form C. 2118.

INTELLIGENCE SUMMARY

(Erase heading not required.)

Instructions regarding War Diaries and Intelligence Summaries are contained in F. S. Regs., Part II. and the Staff Manual respectively. Title Pages will be prepared in manuscript.

Place	Date	Hour	Summary of Events and Information	Remarks and references to Appendices
VOYENNES	1-2-18		Fine day. Batteries resting and training.	
do.	2-2-18		do. do.	
do.	3-2-18		Fine day. Capt.-Lt. Barton M.C. left with 21 men for T.M. Course at the 4th Army School. Received further instructions for the reorganisation of the Divisional T.M. Batteries. The reorganisation is to be reported complete by the 10th inst.	
do.	4-2-18		Fine day. Men were paraded to their new Batteries & surplus staves of V/30 were set aside to await orders as to their disposal.	
do.	5-2-18		Fine morning. Slight rain in afternoon. Received instruction to post 1 Officer, 1 Sgt. 1 Cpl. 1 Bdr. and 15 O.R's including all surplus R.G.A. men to the new XVIII Corps Heavy T.M. Battery. Reorganisation of Batteries postponed one day.	
do.	6-2-18		Fine day. Lieut F.C. Watson M.C. officers detailed for the H.T.M. Battery.	
do.	7-2-18		Fine days. Resting & training new Batteries.	
do.	8-2-18			
do.	9-2-18			
do.	10-2-18		Fine day. Lieut Kershaw went on leave.	
do.	11-2-18		Fine day. Reorganisation reported complete. Received instructions that the T.M. Personnel would move up into the forward area on the 12th inst. One Battery to be attached to 36th Div and the other to 61st Division. Division (later postponed one day)	
do.	12-2-18		Fine day. Capt A.F./Baillie posted to command Y/30 Battery.	
do.	13-2-18		Wet day. X/30 moved by lorry to 36th Div reporting to Sir M.E. for instructions. Y/30 moved by lorry to 61st Div reporting to Div Arty for instruction.	
In line ST QUENTIN FRONT	14-2-18		Fine day. X/30 under orders of 36th Div Arty preparing S.Pts positions. Y/30 under orders of 61st Div Arty establishing a T.M. position in forward area.	

Army Form C. 2118.

WAR DIARY
INTELLIGENCE SUMMARY

(Erase heading not required.)

Place	Date	Hour	Summary of Events and Information	Remarks and references to Appendices
In line F.QUATRIN AREA	15-2-18		Fine day. Batteries working in forward area.	
do.	16-2-18		Beautiful day. D.T.M.O. visited Y/30 Battery.	
do.	17-2-18		Fine day. Batteries working in forward area.	
do.	18-2-18		Fine day. CRA & Bde Major visited Y/30 Battery. D.T.M.O. visited X/30 Battery in 36th Divl area.	
do.	19-2-18		Fine day. Received instructions that 20th Div Arty. would take over a portion of the line at present held by the 36th Div. & 61st Division respectively at 10 am 23rd inst.	
do.	20-2-18		Fine day. Capt A.F.Baillie & 14 men went to Second Army T.M. School for Course.	
do.	21-2-18		Fine day. HQ's moved from OFFOY to HAM.	
do.	22-2-18		Fine day. Dull. D.T.M.O. reconnoitred positions in the Battle area.	
do.	23-2-18		Fine day. Dull.	
do.	24-2-18		Dull day. Work continued in the forward area.	
do.	25-2-18		Dull day. Some rain.	
do.	26-2-18		Fine day. Wet dull.	
do.	27-2-18		Fine in morning, rain later in afternoon. CRA & RD visited the T.M. emplacements with the D.T.M.O. in the afternoon. Received instructions to push on with the emplacements in the forward area with all speed & to put the guns in temporary emplacements.	
do.	28-2-18		Wet cold fine day later. 3 6" T.M. thrash from Corps Ordnance & taken up to positions also 210 rounds of ammunition. Lieut Kershaw returned from leave.	

W.O. Eyre Capt
D.T.M.O. 30 Division

WAR DIARY 30th DIVISION TRENCH MORTAR BATTERIES

INTELLIGENCE SUMMARY

Army Form C. 2118.

Vol 10

Place	Date	Hour	Summary of Events and Information	Remarks and references to Appendices
SAVY (St QUENTIN area)	1-3-18		Still cold day. Work was continued on the T.M. Emplacements in the Forward & Battle area.	
do.	2-3-18		Heavy fall of snow, cold day. Capt. A.F. Baillie and 2Lieut Heber went to Paris to represent the Divisional Rugby Team.	
do.	3-3-18		Cold day, rain & snow at night. Another 6" T.M. + 40 Rounds of ammunition was taken up & placed in position in the Battle Zone.	
do.	4-3-18		Cold wet day. In afternoon A/CRA + Bde Major visited two of the T.M. emplacements being constructed.	
do.	5-3-18		Dull day. Work was continued on emplacements.	
do	6-3-18		Fine day. Two G.S. Wagons were detailed from D.A.C. to bring the surplus stores for X & Y Batteries from VOYENNES to DURY.	
do	7-3-18		Fine day. One 6" T.M. was registered on its Barrage lines from the MANCHESTER HILL REDOUBT.	
do	8-3-18		Much warmer day. Two guns were taken up to Battle positions at X28f-	
do	9-3-18		Fine day. 220 Rounds 6" Ammunition was taken up to Positions in L'EPINE de DALLON & 110 to Positions in BROWN QUARRY.	
do	10-3-18		Fine day. 60 Rounds 6" T.M. Ammunition taken up to Y/30 Battery positions in BATTLE ZONE.	
do	11-3-18		Cloudy warm weather. One 6" T.M. was Ammunition that in action in ROUPY to cover the Battle Zone. The two guns in L'EPINE de DALLON were registered.	
do	12-3-18		Weather beautiful. Work continued in Forward and Battle Emplacements.	
do	13-3-18		Warm warm day. Divisional Gas Officer visited X T.M. Batteries. 50 Rounds 6" ammunition taken up to ROUPY Positions + one Gun driven + put in action in BOSTON QUARRY.	
do	14-3-18		Fine day. Work continued. A/CRA. visited Y/30 emplacements.	
do	15-3-18		Cool day.	

WAR DIARY
or
INTELLIGENCE SUMMARY.
(Erase heading not required.)

Army Form C. 2118.

Place	Date	Hour	Summary of Events and Information	Remarks and references to Appendices
SAVY	16-3-18		This day X/30 Battery moved HQ's to ROUPY.	
do & from	17-3-18		Beautiful day. X/30 Registered his 3 guns in the Battle Zone.	
SAVY & ROUPY	18-3-18		Very warm day. Y/30 registered his two of his guns in the BATTLE ZONE.	
do	19-3-18		D.T.M.O. went on leave. Capt G.H. Barton acting in his absence.	
do	20-3-18		Fine day.	
do	21-3-18		Great bombardment took at along the whole Divnor. front. Orders were given to man Battle the hrs of great intensity. Advanced to attack at 8.30 am against numbers. Stations heavy. Enemy attack penetrated our Battle positions & all guns captured. 2nd Lieut A.W Humphreys the day the enemy had penetrated our Battle positions & all guns captured. 2nd Lieut V.A. Neve with Ten men in to 10 men the L'EPINE DE DALLON Redoubt were missing. 2nd Lieut V.A Neve with Ten men in the MANCHESTER HILL Redoubt fired his ammunition & after the Redoubt was completely surrounded he & his men broke through and got back to the Battle Position. He was wounded in this break. The evacuation of the Batteries were Two Officers & 19 ORs.	
	22-3-18		During this period the officers & men of both Batteries were split up & attached to the	
	23-3-18		148 & 149 (Bdes) & D.A.C.	
	24-3-18			
	25-3-18			
	26-3-18			
	27-3-18			
	28-3-18			
	29-3-18			
	30-3-18			
	31-3-18			

Army Form C. 2118.

WAR DIARY
or
INTELLIGENCE SUMMARY.

(Erase heading not required.)

7TH DIVISION TRENCH MORTAR BATTERIES

Instructions regarding War Diaries and Intelligence Summaries are contained in F. S. Regs., Part II. and the Staff Manual respectively. Title pages will be prepared in manuscript.

Place	Date	Hour	Summary of Events and Information	Remarks and references to Appendices
	1.4.18		During this period the Officers & men of both Batteries were getting up and attached to the 108 & 109 Bde's R.F.A.	Censored
	to			
	30.4.18			

Signed, Brigade Major.
75th (County Palatine) Divisional Artillery.

Army Form C. 2118.

WAR DIARY
or
INTELLIGENCE SUMMARY.

(Erase heading not required.)

  10th (Mounted) Division 1/5/18 to 31/5/18

Place	Date	Hour	Summary of Events and Information	Remarks and references to Appendices
	1.5.18 to 30.5.18		During this period the Officers & men of Hors Batteries were attached to 168 & 149, Bdes RFA & DAC	
	31.5.18		Batteries disbanded. Personnel posted to Bdes & DAC.	

Arthur H...
Brigade Major
10th (County Palatine) Divisional Artillery.

WAR DIARY
INTELLIGENCE SUMMARY
(Erase heading not required.)

Army Form C. 2118.

July 1918

Place	Date	Hour	Summary of Events and Information	Remarks and references to Appendices
	1.7.18		Trench Mortar Batteries reformed. Lt. P. Heenan rejoins 30 T.M.Bn and is placed in command of 30 T.M.Br. 90 reinforcements received, a great number of the old T.M. Personnel volunteer for further service. Mjr A. Shepherd posted from 30 O.A.C. to T.M.Bs.	
	2.7.18			
	3.7.18			
	4.7.18			
	5.7.18		Training of new personnel. Lewis Gun & Rifle since Ela	
	6.7.18			
	7.7.18			
	8.7.18			
	9.7.18		2Lt. L.G. Madden posted from 30 D.A.C. to Y/30. 2Lt. F.G. Mascott posted from 30 DAC to X/30. 2Lt. O. Sarbard posted to X/30 from D30.	
	10.7.18		Lt. D.R. Thornton posted from 30 RAC to Y/30. 2 0.0B.	
	11.7.18		Batteries training	
	12.7.18		2Lt J. Shaels posted to X/30 from B.	
	13.7.18			
	14.7.18		Batteries training	
	15.7.18		Capt. P. Heenan assumed CRA to the line to reconnoitre the positions.	
	16.7.18		Lt. E.L. Armstrong posted to Y/30 from 30 DAC. 2Lt. J. Wilkinson posted to X/30 from 30 BAC.	
	17.7.18		Batteries went in to take & position neuve position. 2Lt L.S. Martin proceeds at Capt. to command X/30. Lieut. from 18/7/18.	
	18.7.18		S.O passed and qualified to Second Army Junior School for course in 6" N.J.	
	19.7.18			
	20.7.18		Y/30. all completed & ready for action X/30 still completed and ready for action	X/30. R.19. a. 2040. (3 mortars)
	21.7.18		Batteries in present position	R.20.a. 90.10 (3 mortars)
	22.7.18			Y/30. R.21. a. 1080 (3 mortars)
	23.7.18			
	24.7.18			
	25.7.18			
	26.7.18			
	27.7.18			
	28.7.18			
	29.7.18		Capt. P. Heenan relinquished & ET.M.O. appointed by GHQ auth A.G.7157/7004 (c) GHQ 4-29/7	
	30.7.18			
	31.7.18		Notes of appointment from 30 Barricks J Q by B/11490 of 31/7/18	

WAR DIARY of TRENCH MORTAR BATTERIES 30TH DIVISIONAL ARTILLERY

INTELLIGENCE SUMMARY
(Erase heading not required.) August 1918.

Army Form C. 2118.

Place	Date	Hour	Summary of Events and Information	Remarks and references to Appendices
In the Field	1		Batteries in position, fine weather	
	2		D.T.M.O. interviewed O.C. T.M.O. 35th Div. and their position with a view to taking over	
	3		Fine day	
	4		Fine day	
	5		D.T.M.O. accompanied C.R.A. up line to reconnoitre position in forward area	
	6		Fine day	
	7		Fine day. O.S.C. Batteries reconnoitred 35th Div. positions	
	8		D.T.M.O. went up line to prepare for relief, visiting B.C⁰⁵	
	9		Fine day	
	10		Fine day. relieved 35th Div. T.M.	
	11		D.T.M.O. and Battery Commanders went up line to reconnoitre new positions in forward area	
	12		Fine day. 100 rounds 6" T.M. Ammunition taken up to positions	
	13		Fine day. D.T.M.O. went up line to interview Battery Commander. 100 rds 6" T.M. amm taken up	
	14		Fine day. Preparing positions in forward area. M.S.d. 30.18. Infantry only course in Rigging Room	
	15		Fine day. Special positions forward ready for action	
	16		Fine day. D.T.M.O. went up line to inspect rear positions. Final arrangements for Heratium	
	17		Fine day. D.T.M.O. visited Battery Commander O.C. X/30 & 2/L J. Wilkinson in Charge	
	18		Dull weather. Hurricane Bombardment in divisional front, 90 rounds fired in conjunction with operation 21/30 promised (Successful)	
	19–25		Showery turning to heavy rain	
	26		D.T.M.O. visited Battery Commanders	
	27			
	28			
	29		Battery Commanders reconnoitred forward area for T.M. positions for 4th Batteries worth class a during Enemy withdrawal	
	30			
	31			

D.T.M.O.
30TH
DIVL. ARTILLERY.

WAR DIARY / INTELLIGENCE SUMMARY

TRENCH MORTAR BATTERIES
30TH DIVISIONAL ARTILLERY
SEPTEMBER 1918

Army Form C. 2118.

Place	Date	Hour	Summary of Events and Information	Remarks and references to Appendices
	1		Fine day	
	2		Fine day	
	3		D.T.M.O. moved HQ quarters from Godowaersvelde to R.E.C. Central	
	4		Fine day. Batteries moved from R.E.C. to fields near the village of Pradelle	
	5		Fine day	
	6		Fine day. D.T.M.O. went up line to interview B.C's. V/30 fired 14 rounds on Strong point at N.36.6.60.50	
	7		Fine day. D.T.M.O. went up line to interview B.C's in positions covering Doulieu. V/30 fired 18 rds at Strong point N 36.6.60.50	
	8		Dull rainy day. V/30 fired 26 rounds on Special targets at request of Infantry	
	9		Wet morning. D.T.M.O. went up line to interview B.C's. V/30 fired at target pointed out by OC Infantry	
	10		Fine day	
	11		Dull day. Evening fine. D.C V/30 came from Leave to conter B.T.M.O. re new position on line. V/30 fired 22 rds into enemy trenches	
	12		Very wet day. V/30 fired 25 rounds into enemy post, Crater in N.36.a	
	13		Dull day. V/30 fired 20 rounds into Crater in N.36.a and enemy posts. X/30 fired 10 rounds into Ontario Farm, V.1.a	
	14		Dull day. V/30 fired 13 rounds on Crater in N.36.a. X/30 fired 10 rounds on Ontario Farm. D.T.M.O went up line to interview B.C's and recce O.P's	
	15		Fine day. Battery fired 40 rounds harassing fire on Crater in N.36.a. Ontario Farm.	
	16		Fine day. On the night of the 15/16 X/30 were withdrawn from action, during the afternoon and evening V/30 V/30 were withdrawn	
	17		During this period the batteries were resting awaiting instructions	
	18		B.T.M.O. visited II Corps for orders. Batteries moved to the vicinity of Elverdinghe. Where also was recently taken	
	19		Batteries attached to II Corps. Administered by 119 AFA Bde RFA. Attached to DA-Arty. D.T.M.O will B.S.M. T.M. Officer (brigaded limited)	
	20		D.T.M.O with Battery Commander reconnoitred You positions accompanied by Captain, commandant & Hav. spare in charge of T.M's. 3 ST. mortar teams forward to 20 S.W. 4/4/15.d. B.T.M.O arranges ammunition supply, one new ammunition by shell delivery	
	21		All mortar forward. 4 mortar teams get ready for action. Belgian infantry paid to supply ammunition	
	22		All mortar in action. Going very difficult owing to rain. 1200 rounds forward	
	23		450 rounds at Gun positions. Gun mounted and slipped to enemy ammunition. 300 infantry supplied to carry bombs	
	24		1600 rounds at Gun positions. R.O.C./Morton wounded. Postmortem trestle recovered. Felthurn town formed Offensive fire at 2.32 a.m. Barrage lasted for 3 hour. Infantry attack at 5.30 am. 1445 rounds, these wait excellent results. Very wet.	
	25		Guns pulled out. Mortar instruction from 2 Corp. Go letter to Burrows very wet weather.	
	26		Return 16 30 rds. V/30 attached to 161 section DTMC	
	27		B.T.M.O T.V./30 attached to No 2 section DAC	

B.T.M.O. 30TH DIV. ARTILLERY

No 17

War Diary

Trench Mortar Batteries

30th Div Arty

October 1918

Volume

WAR DIARY or INTELLIGENCE SUMMARY

Army Form C. 2118.

TRENCH MORTAR BATTERIES
30TH DIVISIONAL ARTILLERY
OCTOBER 1918

Place	Date	Hour	Summary of Events and Information	Remarks and references to Appendices
In the Field	1/10/18		During this period the batteries were attached to 30th D.A.C.	
	2			
	3			
	4		Dull morning. D.T.M.O. & O.C. T/30 went up line to Neermolen	
	5		T/30 prepared position on S/15 h.000 P.18.a.80.40. 30/30 attacked 305 T.M.E.	
	6		T/30 returned to wagon line & waited 24 hours	
	7		T/30 prepared position for wire cutting in P.14.a.20.80. S/28 SE 136 rds ammunition taken to position	
	8		T/30 commenced wire cutting under the supervision of O.C. in Q.19.c.00.70 Q.19.c.40.00 Q.19.c.99.00 S'Indr expend 153 rds fired	
	9		Wire cutting continued by T/30 150 rds expended 40 rds taken F position C position	
	10		" " " T/30 " 88 " " " 40 " " . D.T.M.O took up residence at H.Q.D.A.	
	1		Dull wet morning. T/30 returned 6 wagon teams	
	2		10-T.M.O Fired 100 Rounds in Connection with opening attack.	
	3		T/30 Returned to wagon line. T/30 following them very wet — heavy enemy shelling	
	4		Rained heavily. D.T.M.O proceeded on leave to UK. OC T/30 2/Lt DMD (acting) Lieu Battery moved to Q.Bd.37(B) 3	
	5		Fine. CRA inspected mortars & new mobile carriages	
	6		Fine. Orders given by CRA for T/30 to join Hvy. Trench Mortar Bat'ry during Relief	
	7		Showery. 15/30 joined 8/148 Inde. T/1/8 ? at 2/149 Bde.	
	8		" 15/30 fired 12 Mortars (Grenade Rifle) in WELCHIN. Banks shoot participating.	
	9		Enemy fired heavy trench mortar in WELCHIN area.	
20	1		15/30 fired 23 rounds (on target) in tearing fire. Enemy Rifles ? opened our positions	
	2		Quiet day	
	3		15/30 fired 15 rounds harrowing fire. Slight retaliation	
	4		Double hostile fired upon by enemy. One unobserved battery at Heldrich	
	5		Quiet day. 15/30 withdrawn from line	
	6		Enjoy all day at rest	
	7		Quiet day	
	8			
	9			
30				
	1		D2 M. O Returned from leave	

Signature — Captain H.L.
D.T.M.O. 30th Div. Arty

www.ingramcontent.com/pod-product-compliance
Lightning Source LLC
Chambersburg PA
CBHW081455160426
43193CB00013B/2494